THE STORY OF QUEEN'S PARK BRIGHTON

BRIGHTON TOWN PRESS

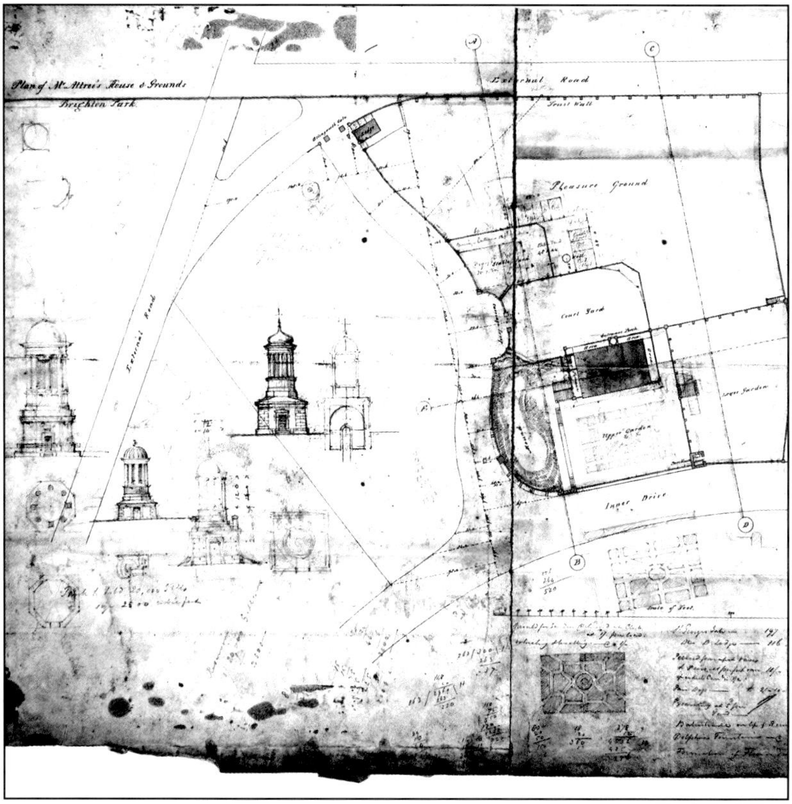

Charles Barry's drawings for the Pepperbox and plan for Attree villa circa 1828

Contents

Cover: *Charles Barry's vision for the villas surrounding Brighton Park*

Inside front cover: *portrait of Thomas Attree*

both images reproduced with the kind permission of Howlett Clarke solicitors

Inside back cover: *The Clock Tower in snow 2007 courtesy the Argus*

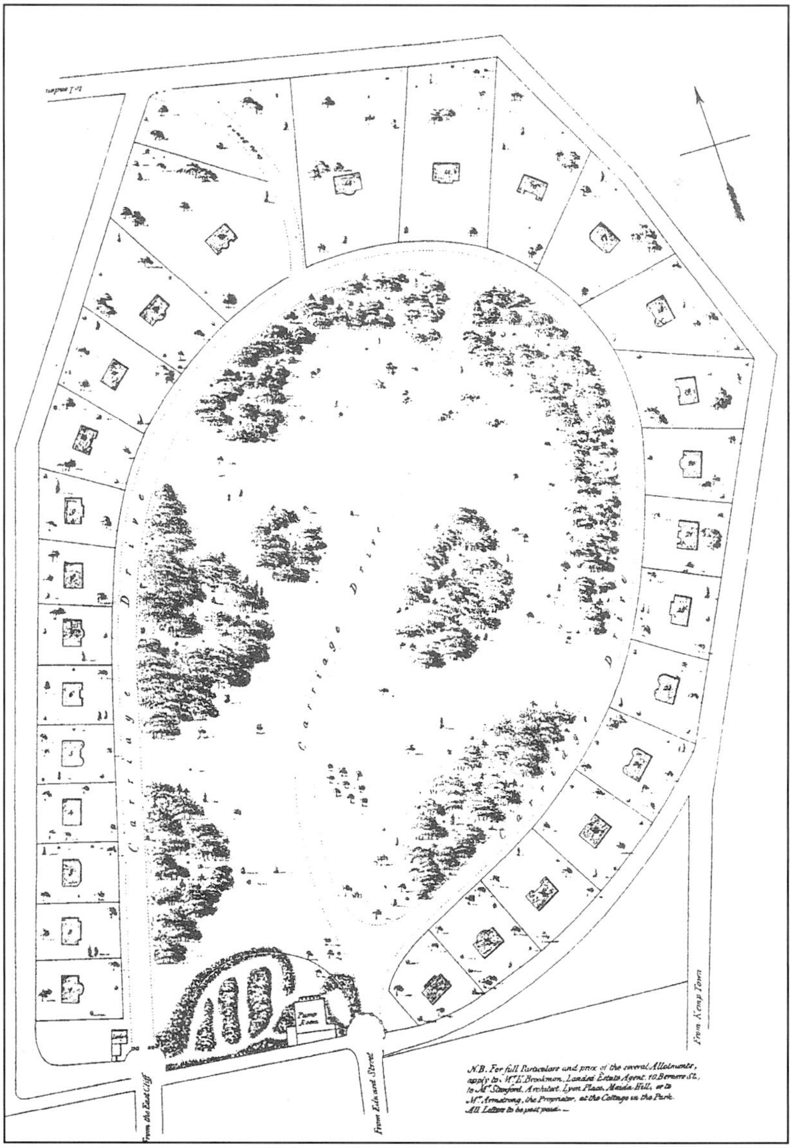

John Armstrong's 1822 plan was to create a garden overlooked by substantial villas

Introduction

Like many parks Queen's Park is an amalgam of two histories, one private and one public. Its origin, as the setting for grand villas, sprang from the same speculative imperative as some of our finest town landscapes – John Nash's Regents Park in London (begun in 1811), Joseph Paxton's Birkenhead Park on the Wirral and, more modestly, James Burton's St Leonards Gardens in Hastings. All were laid out in the Picturesque style popularised by Humphrey Repton and Nash with serpentine paths weaving through undulating ground planted with islands of mixed trees, shrubbery and flowers, now hiding, now revealing vistas. The style would have been high fashion to John Armstrong who first planted the Park in the early 1820s; possibly inspired by Nash's picuresque Royal Pavilion gardens which were completed at that time.

Serpentine paths weaving through undulating ground...

The Park's second history began in 1890 and from contemporary accounts it seems that the Corporation's Head Gardener and Surveyor appreciated and retained the beauty of the site, though adding copious new plantings,winding paths and water. They recognized, as did other towns, how picturesque character is well suited to public parks in bringing a sense of the countryside and horticultural variety into street-bound lives. Brighton used to be proud of its staff's horticultural expertise and never sought advice.

Queen's Park today retains much of its 19th century character - indeed its beauty depends greatly on that. While its topography has allowed necessary facilities to be discreetly sited, perhaps a missing feature is its picturesque shrubbery. Cost is always a factor but volunteers at the Pavilion have a wonderful time gardening the shrubberies there. This book removes any excuse for us not fully appreciating the park's design and importance in social and garden history; it should prove invaluable in guiding its future.

Virginia Hinze: English Heritage SE Regional Landscape Architect

Attree Villa, steel engraving 1835. The Pepperpot and a gateway are visible behind the Villa, the gazebo and Italian garden terraces are in the foreground

Preamble

The Mayor was a happy man. He had been to many events in bad weather recently, but today the sun was shining gloriously. A brisk breeze off the sea made the flags flutter bravely, though it meant that gentlemen had to keep a hand on their tall hats. He looked around with a sense of satisfaction, at the assembled Aldermen and Councillors, the local Member of Parliament Gerald Loder, the Race Course Trustees and the specially invited guests in the roped-off enclosure inside the high gates. Through the gates he could see a large crowd stretching down Egremont Place, of the poor people from down near the cliffs and the even poorer people of the dank slums on the shoulder of the hill towards the Steine. To amuse everyone whilst they waited Mr Trussell's String Band sawed away, accompanied by a choir from the Chailey Industrial School.

The opening ceremony performed by the Mayor, Sir J Ewart

On the dot of midday the Mayor stepped forward. One of the Race Course Trustees handed him a key, and with the words 'That the gateways be now thrown open and the Park dedicated to the use and enjoyment of the public for ever' he turned the key and willing hands pulled them open. Retaining as much dignity as possible before the surging crowd the Mayor, accompanied by his mace-bearer, his chaplain and his piper in full Highland rig, made his way to the other six iron gates where similar formalities took place.

He then processed to the side of the newly built lake where, on a crimson carpeted platform, there were prayers, speeches and a tree was planted. The dignitaries then retired for a hearty lunch, leaving the Park to the people of Brighton who swarmed all over it for the rest of the day.

The date was 10th August, 1892, but Queen's Park had had over 70 years of history before that date.

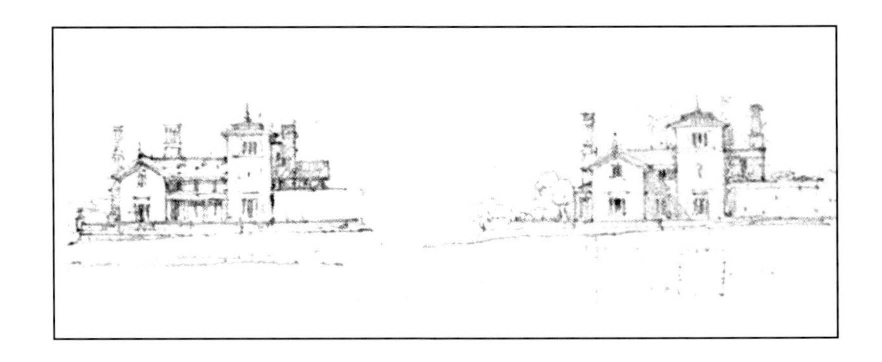

Charles Barry's sketches for the design of Attree Villa

1 History

The early history of the Park is really one of property development, with the gardens as the bait. Back in 1820 it was just an unspoilt downland valley to the north of the creeping sections of housing speculatively put up nearer the sea. Egremont Place was a typical example. But Brighton was on the verge of a major building boom. Between 1820 and 1830 the number of houses in the town doubled to about 8,000. This was the period that saw the creation of most of the squares, crescents and terraces that make Brighton so distinctive today.

The valley was agricultural land, almost all of it broken up into the system of laines and furlongs of the medieval land tenure system. To John Armstrong in 1822 this valley seemed ripe for development, and at the end of that year he acquired a lease on it. That lease covered an area about four times that of the present Park. Little is known about Armstrong, though newspapers of the time referred to his 'known experience and judgement in landscape gardening'. His plan was to create a garden overlooked by plots of land for substantial villas, the profit coming from the sale of those plots. The garden would be for the exclusive use of the villa owners.

In January 1823 the Brighton Gazette carried a report that 'fifty acres of ground are to be enclosed and laid out for tea and pleasure gardens, a kind of Vauxhall'. Two weeks later it embarrassingly had to report that what was actually intended bore 'no resemblance to a tea-garden but will assume the character of a park'. It described a terrace with a fine view of the sea and a half mile carriage drive 'through a richly ornamented scene'.

Armstrong managed to get George IV on board, to the extent that the King was shown the plans and 'expressed approbation of them'. By winter 1824 advertisements were appearing for

EDWARD FOX

Edward Fox (1823-1899) was the son of a landscape artist of the same name. The father had made drawings of Brighton and the surroundings in its heydayin the early part of the 19th century. The son also saw himself as an artist , though working in the then new medim of photography.

The younger Fox achieved recognition nationally for his talents, and for some fifty years recorded Brighton's seafront, buildings, churches and streets. The quality of his composition can be seen in the lithograph opposite, on page 13

'Brighton Park', and spoke of a Pump Room being in the grounds. At the same time the plots of land were offered for sale 'for the erection of detached villas', which 'commanded an uninterrupted view of the varied scenery of the Park, the Downs and the Sea'. In the following summer of 1825 an unmetalled roadway was made from Edward Street to the lower entrance to make for easier access, and soon after the Duke and Duchess of Gloucester drove round the Park to give it a further royal imprimatur.

At this time the Gazette described the grounds as 'assuming a most delightful appearance now the plants and shrubs begin to attain their growth. It forms a very pleasant drive and the German Spa at the southern end is much frequented'. Until the money flowed in from the plot sales Armstrong sought to make an income by allowing the public in on payment of a substantial annual subscription of a guinea (worth nearly £50 today). However for a single visit only threepence was demanded, and for a further tuppence a nosegay would be picked and presented to carry away.

Despite this Armstrong's hopes proved illusory. He was soon unable to find the rent to pay Thomas Kemp, the principal landowner, and he was possibly not helped by a bank panic at the end of 1825. Armstrong seems to have been very much under-capitalised for such a venture. On his plan for the park he states that the 'price of the several Allotments of land can be found by contacting him at the cottage in the park', but carefully stipulates that all letters were to be post paid - hardly an indication of substantial resources. After only two years, in early 1826, the land is in other ownership. It is not clear exactly how this happened. One story was that Armstrong had died, another that the land was initially split up into many small plots intended for cultivation and yet another that Thomas Attree bought the whole place, but certainly soon afterwards the entire area was owned jointly by Messrs Attree, Mighell and Kemp.

Messrs Attree, Mighell and Kemp were substantial landowners in the town and in Armstrong's valley and had collaborated previously on speculative building.

2 Attree's Ownership

Lithograph of 1863 by Waterlow & Sons taken from an original photograph by Edward Fox

Attree was a major figure in the town, known by his enemies as the 'King of Brighton', a solicitor who, like his father, handled the Royal family's affairs locally. He was Clerk, Solicitor and Treasurer to the Vestry, the Commissioners and the Poor Law Guardians. Many of his appointments were ended when the administration of the town was altered in 1825, but he retained some and remained a power locally.

The second of the trio, Thomas Read Kemp, developed Kemp Town until bankruptcy drove him abroad to a pauper's death in Paris. He was by far the biggest contributor of the three. Mighell had acquired land in many parts of the town and had a hand in many of its property developments of the time. In 1892 the Mayor said these three 'met together for the purpose of rescuing these beautiful grounds which lent themselves so much to ornamentation'.

THE VESTRY

From the late 18th century the town was run by three groups, the Vestry, the Commssioners and the High Constable. There were regular disputes between them, not infrequently ending up in the Courts.

In very broad terms the Vestry of about forty members approximated to today's Council and was the most important of the bodies. During its life it pronounced on many issues - civil liberties, national taxes, electoral reform, the railway, etc. It showed a consistently liberal - and at times distinctly radical - bias.

The Commissioners, up to a hundred of them, covered what we would see today as the Borough Engineer's remit - roads, lighting and, especially for them, the groynes. The High Constable covered law and order. Each office had some sort of election, but they were far from direct elections and certainly not universal.

Modest stipends were paid, in the case of the High Constable it was10 guineas per year (about half of which went on the Annual Dinner).

All this came to an end in 1854 when the town was incorporated.

Published by
German

A fashionable archery club near the Spa building, southern end, 'well-sheltered, embanked at both ends for safety and with a rustic club house'.

THE ATTREE FAMILY

Thomas Attree was the son of William Attree, who set up a solicitor's practice at 8 Ship Street in the late 1760s, just as Dr Russell was beginning to promote the virtues of sea-bathing and change Brighthelmstone for ever. William Attree was the first Clerk to the Vestry - and to the Commissioners too - from 1773 until 1810, when Thomas inherited those offices.

Another son Harry turned to journalism and authorship and founded the 'Brighton Herald' in 1806 which, due to the closeness to the Court, was the first newspaper in the country to announce the victory of Trafalgar. William founded a dynasty and the Attree family are still active in the town today.

This joint ownership did not last long, for by 1830 it is plain that Attree owned the land alone. Feeling he had outgrown his modest family home in Ship Street where he had been born, Attree sought a new residence reflecting his elevated position - a miniature country house on the edge of town - and promptly commissioned up-and-coming Charles Barry to design it. Attree retained the notion of selling the other building plots, having already dabbled in property development by building Marine Square in 1824. There is a charming watercolour and a lithograph of the scheme as visualised in 1834 (shown on the cover of this book), showing a noble sweep of large detached houses in a surprising range of styles overlooking the central grounds. Among the villas is the newly-built Attree Villa, with gazebo and the Pepperpot behind it, and alongside it to the westward the only known view of the very first villa that was erected - Cowell's Villa.

The description below the watercolour provides more details. 'The building Plots are confined to the space between the Upper Drive and the Boundary Wall. They contain an average depth of 250 feet, and may have any amount of frontage as desired. The owner of each plot is at liberty to build according to his Design, subject to the approval of the Proprietor. The interior of the Park within the Drive is not to be built upon, but left free and for ever appropriated for lawn and Plantations. The trees of the latter are of ten years growth'. This type of plan owes more to developments like Calverley Park in Tunbridge Wells than the contemporary developments in Brighton of sweeping crescents and formal squares, from which it is quite different.

Attree's first step was to build the boundary wall all round the grounds, and that wall still forms the back garden wall of the villas in West Drive. The only structures at this time were the entrance gateways and lodges, along with the Spa. The first domestic building to go up was built by a Mr Cowell around 1830, but around 1845 this was transformed, either by demolition or major development, into the much larger Pennant Lodge that is now known as Queen's Park Villa. The next house to appear was Attree Villa, with the Pepperpot. By 1836 Attree had capitalised on his royal connections to give the whole area the name of Queen's Park, in honour of Queen Adelaide, wife of William IV. He retained those connections to the end of his life, the Duchess of Cambridge and her daughter, the future Queen Mary, visiting him in his villa in the year of his death.

Pennant Lodge built in 1845, now known as Queen's Park villa

Another royal visitor to the gardens was Victoria, but only fleetingly. For this event the lower gateway was decorated with a huge VR made of dahlias, a Union Jack was raised from a flagpole set on the lawn of the Royal Spa, and 'Mr Thomas Attree's Belvedere Tower' was illuminated with flambeaux in the evening. On the Saturday after her arrival in Brighton the Queen managed to fit in a visit to the park and huge crowds assembled at the gates in anticipation. She drove up to Queen's Park in her carriage, but then drove straight through and out of the northern entrance, re-entering the town by the Lewes Road and leaving the crowd with nothing to huzza.

The Park in the 1840s was described by a Dr Granville as 'the only decent plantation to be seen in or near Brighton, the rest are dismal-looking, barren and discouraging'. It boasted a fashionable archery club near the Spa building at the southern end, 'well-sheltered, embanked at both ends for safety and with a rustic clubhouse'. Archery fêtes held there in 1839 raised over £44 for the new Adelaide Wing at the County Hospital. The only visitors normally to the grounds would have been Attree's guests, but during such fêtes the grounds were thrown open to the public. This secluded tone of the area, with rare public access, remained the norm through the 1850s into the 1860s and Attree's death.

Duddell's Villa and Grounds in 1894 showing: gardener's cottage, kitchen garden, orchard with peach house and vinery, tennis court, Italian garden, stabling, lodge and the Pepperpot

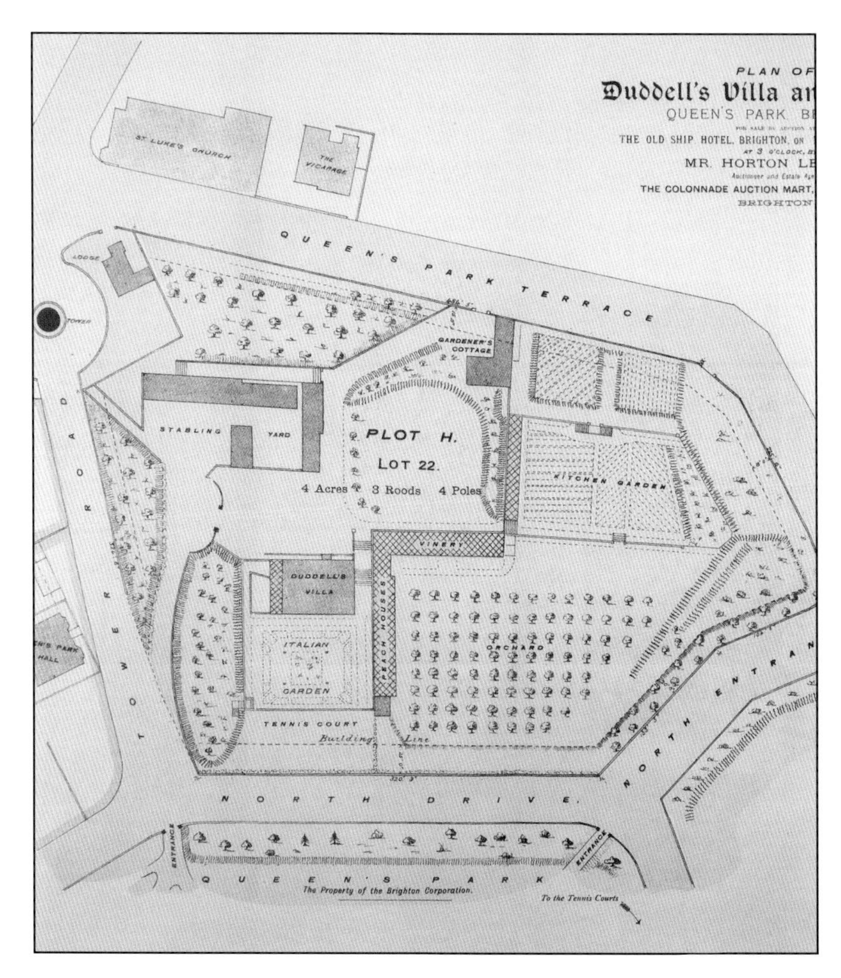

Below: advertisement for The Tower Press which Duddell helped his relative set up in the Pepperpot

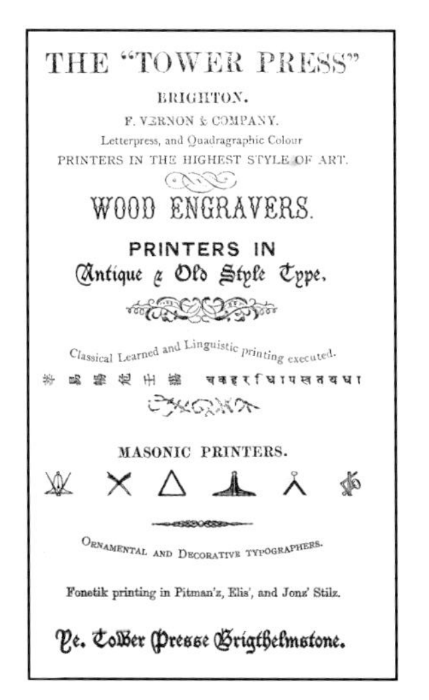

3 Duddell's Ownership

The next stage in the story of Queen's Park centres around a George Duddell, of Parliament Street in London. He was a very colourful character, having made a modest fortune as one of the earliest pioneers in the tough commercial free-for-all of Hong Kong, but the money he used to buy the Attree estate was in fact borrowed from a wealthy widow, a Mrs Blake, who, with her husband, had been close friends in the Far East. The estate was auctioned in 1863 at a total valuation of some £40,000, made up of £30,000 for the Park, £6,000 for Attree's villa, and all other buildings for £4,000. However it was knocked down for only £28,000 of the widow's money - equivalent to around £1,250,000 today. This was despite the auctioneer's description of it as 'within ten minutes of the sea, standing high and in immediate proximity of the healthiest part of the town. The roads are arranged so as to leave the highest and best parts of the property for building purposes and, from the great scarcity of detached villas in Brighton, there can be no doubt that residences of that class erected here would meet with ready tenants at highly remunerative rents'. But hedging their bets the auctioneers also said the estate could provide Brighton with a public park.

Something about the turn of events made one local newspaper say 'we have little doubt the estate will soon be before the public again as a Joint Stock Company, a Brighton Building Company or it may be cut up into lots and plots. At any rate rumour is saying that the whole estate is more likely to be speedily adorned with human habitations than converted into a haunt of pleasure or retained as the fair garden of Flora'. Fortunately such gloomy prophecies proved wrong and the central garden grounds remained. However Duddell did turn the archery grounds into a giant roller skating rink and sold off some considerable sections of the land during his twenty odd years of ownership.

GEORGE DUDDELL

Duddell first went to Burma where he made a fortune whilst still in his teens, then lost it due to offending the Government and having it all confiscated. He moved on to Hong Kong, arriving a bare two years after the flag was raised and a year after formal cession of the Colony. He soon became the third largest owner of land there. In 1857 the 'Arrow' war broke out with China, the local Chinese retaliated by trying to poison all the colonists and Duddell was singled out. In fear of his life he fled the Colony the following year.

Duddell kept a close eye on his Hong Kong properties from England, but also ventured into setting up cattle ranches in the empty north of Australia, driving cattle there from southern Queensland. This was the heroic period of Australian droving. There are hills in the Northern Territory today named after the men he sent out. Duddell also bought land on Vancouver Island in Western Canada and in Vancouver itself, when these places were just being opened up. In short he was the classic Victorian Empire venturer.

Duddell funded these projects from the rents of his Hong Kong properties. Having returned with a fortune of only £3,500 (worth £150,000 today), he was obliged to borrow money for the Attree Estate from Mrs Blake, who was immensely rich. At one time he owed her £70,000 (in 1860 money).

From the 'Particulars of Sale' of Queen's Park, 1863

He also moved into Attree's villa with his elderly mother, an illegitimate son from Hong Kong and an orphaned niece named Sophy with her four children. Though surnamed Vernon the gossip was that the children were actually his. Three more children were born to Sophy, and astonishingly the last was near the time that his resident orphaned great niece, Kate Dubois, also produced a child. Kate went on to provide Duddell with three more children. Sophy understandably decamped to London in dudgeon and married a clerk, by who she had more offspring. Despite their 32 year difference in ages Duddell eventually married Kate. And in spite of his extraordinary love life - fairly remarkable today but even more so in Victorian times - Duddell lived a very social life, hosting dinner parties and having thirteen servants to attend his needs. Brighton society in the 1870s was plainly quite broad-minded.

Duddell was well regarded by many as generous and charitable, a friend of the working classes, and he was on the boards of other local benevolent organisations. But others of a conservative bent saw him as a 'distasteful individual'. Elected as a Liberal to the Town Council, on one occasion on being howled down he climbed on the table and harangued the Councillors from there. Having published a newspaper in Hong Kong, he also published his own newspaper for the town, the Brighton Mail, from the Pepperpot.

It is clear that the grounds as well as Attree's Villa itself were let run to seed somewhat during Duddell's ownership. When he died in 1887 the estate was again auctioned but it failed to sell despite the auctioneer suggesting that the Villa had been built by William IV for Queen Adelaide. By this time, in the last quarter of the nineteenth century, the idea of public parks was taking hold. The Borough Corporation tried to purchase the centre of the estate to make a public park, but Duddell's widow declined to name a price on the grounds that if the Corporation rejected it no one else would offer as much.

4 Corporation Ownership

Into this stalemate stepped the Race Course Trustees. These had been self-appointed after the races had fallen to a very low ebb around 1850. They built a new stand, persuaded both the Railway Company and the Queen to give Cups for competition and sought subscriptions from all and sundry. Slowly they turned things around, and by the 1880s were in a sufficiently sound financial position to be able to purchase Tenantry Down (on the Race Hill) and present it to the town. They then looked around for another such project, and their eyes fell on the Attree estate. Painfully drawn-out negotiations with Mrs Duddell ensued. One of the Trustees later said the memory of the negotiations 'made him shudder', and in their report they jointly said 'never before have four gentlemen experienced so much difficulty in giving away £13,500 for the public good'. At a congratulatory banquet for them in 1890 they were each given a silver salver, tea tray and clock worth over £200. One of them, Alderman Riddle, died just before the banquet and it was decided to install a drinking fountain in the Park in his memory.

New Villa, derelict when photographed in 1963 and later demolished

It was the conclusion of these negotiations that eventually provided the reason for the Grand Opening in August 1892 already described. Mrs Duddell retained the plots around the edge of the estate, the Corporation bought the gardens in the middle, a total of 17 acres, plus the Pepperpot. A building line for Mrs Duddell was agreed upon, and a minimum value of the houses to be built. She was as keen on the restrictions as the Corporation since they enhanced the chances of selling the building plots. At this time, even after seventy years on the market, there were still only three of the thirty six available plots actually built on. These three contained Home Lodge, Pennant Lodge and its adjacent New Villa, later Queen's Park Hall, now long gone. The plots were offered

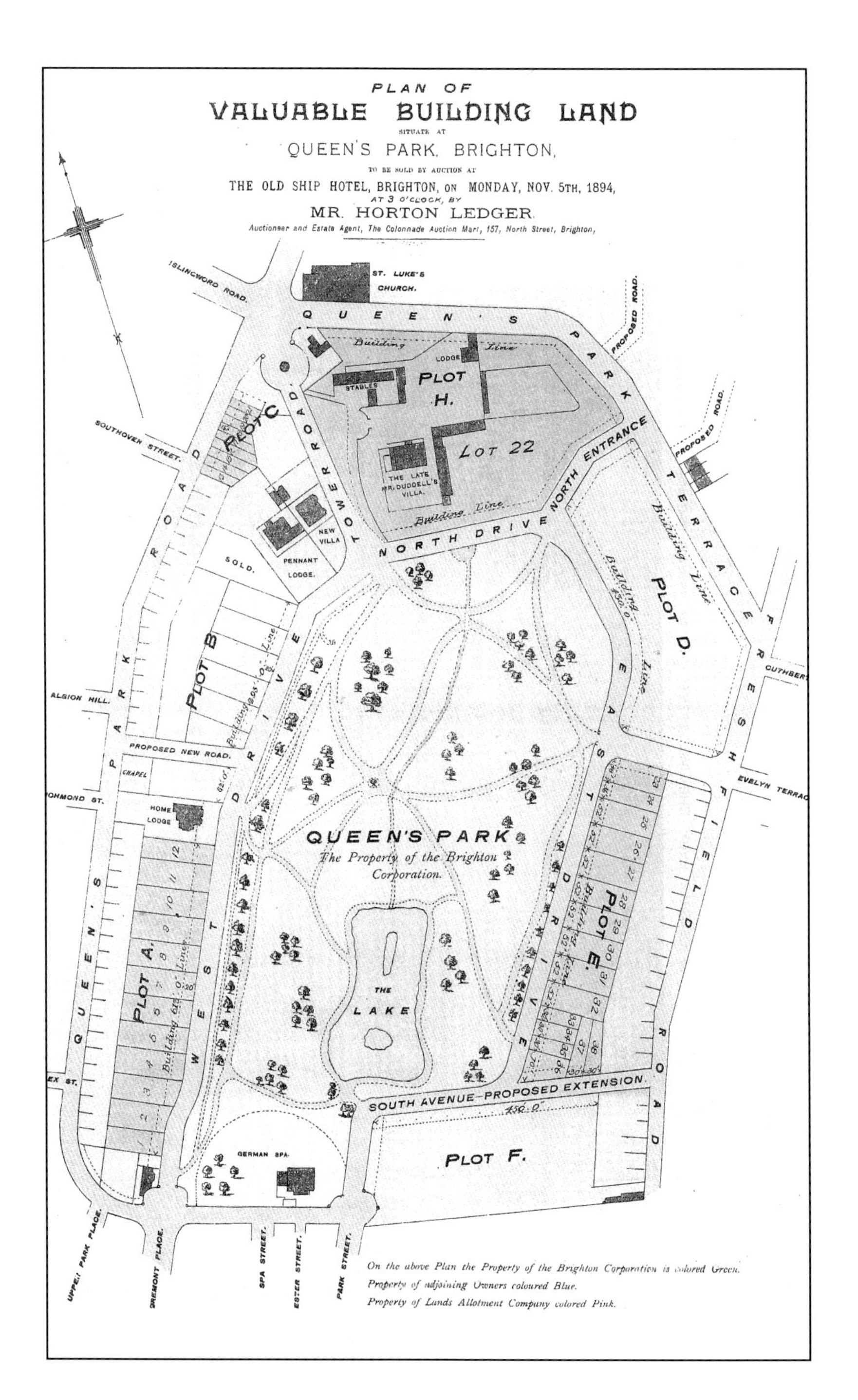

Plan of Queen's Park and surrounding development land from the auctioneer's brochure of 1894

freehold, unlike those earlier in the century which were all leasehold. Two sizeable chunks of land sold by Duddell, on each northerly shoulder of the gardens area, were already in other hands but remained undeveloped. Kate Duddell sold the residue to the Lands Allotment Company Ltd, which promptly went into liquidation. The auctioneer's brochure for this resale surprisingly portrayed the Park that the land overlooked as a romantic estate dotted with waterfalls and inhabited by sheep. Although now in Corporation hands the park was still held out as bait to the purchaser!

The Corporation first had a great deal of work to do on the gardens, not just repairing the laxness of Duddell's stewardship but also laying out roads and sewers and installing gas and water supplies, along with considerable levelling to make access easier. The Corporation Gardener, Mr Ward, drew up extensive plans for the new Park with the help of Francis May, the Borough Engineer and Surveyor. Ward provided weekly reports on progress to the Recreation Gardens Committee and these reports show the astonishing amount of work done. In April 1891 three bushels of grass seed were purchased and two acres of turf imported from Patcham. Swans and Muscovy ducks followed soon after, as did a large donation of rudd, roach and other fish for the new lake from the Sussex Piscatorial Society. Two park keepers were appointed. All the while huge amounts of earth were being moved around which, whilst retaining the general contours, 'left scarcely a foot of the surface undisturbed'. Large flower beds were dug, one and a half miles of footways laid and a mile of elegant railings erected. Some 15,000 trees and shrubs were planted. It was a huge undertaking, taking nearly two years to complete.

Previews of the new Park were given to the Press on the eve of the formal opening, and their reports speak of 'a total transformation, making the Park difficult to recognise as the wilderness it had been a year before'. It was felt that the sterling work of May and Ward had created the feeling that it 'was an old and well-kept private park rather than a public pleasure ground'. In part this was because of its situation in a basin of the Downs with many views of the sea. A major feature of the new Park was the lake, of serpentine shape with two islets and an imitation beach of pebbles, occupying the site of the former roller skating rink installed by Duddell twenty years earlier. The lake was of cement construction, only 2 feet six inches deep and was confidently said to be securely watertight. Sadly time proved that wrong. It received its supply from the main at the Pepperpot, which was let out into a 'most picturesque imaginable rivulet' which meandered through the Park with two small cascades and a couple of rustic bridges to cross it, all the inspiration of Francis May. The ducks took up residence on the islets. It was hoped that in winter the lake would provide splendid

Children in the Park, by George Ruff junior who took many such photographs around Brighton circa 1900

5 The Edwardian Park

So the new Park was built and opened, but inevitably problems soon emerged. Reading between the lines of press reports it seems that things got a little out of hand occasionally, despite the efforts of the Park Keepers. 'Juveniles' gave the swans and ducks a hard time, transferred most of the pebbles from the imitation beach into the lake itself and persistently carved their names on the trunks of the trees. Within a week there were complaints about the rubbish strewn everywhere, a Mrs Lofting demanded compensation for her child's injuries sustained from an iron hurdle, and a Harry Briggs assaulted one of the Park Keepers. Quite a lively opening week.

The first winter saw the lake indeed being frozen over and the Head Gardener reported he swept and scraped the ice and covered it over to provide a good surface. After checking the thickness of ice - between 3 and 4 inches - the public were allowed on it. About 800 people enjoyed the skating that day, and similar numbers on the following two days. The north end was kept for sliders and the south for the skaters. On the Friday the Gardener rigged up lanterns for evening skating, but on the Saturday disaster struck as, with well over a thousand people on the ice, it started to give way so had to be rapidly cleared.

The next year, 1893, the drinking fountain in memory of Alderman Riddle was dedicated, and the names of the Head Gardener and the Borough Surveyor who had done so much to bring the Park into being were justly added as well. With that the Park left behind its chequered history of ownership by developers and entered on its life as a public space, which it retains over 100 years later.

The Park in 1890 would be both strange and familiar to us today. The approach would be strange, for a walk up narrow and tenement-lined Edward Street as it then was would not be something to be lightly considered. The land around the northern

Another photograph of local children in the Park by George Ruff junior

edge of the Park would look strangely undeveloped. St Luke's church and vicarage would be the only buildings to the north of the Park, though work on the first two houses of Queen's Park Terrace was about to get underway. Where St Luke's School stands today was open ground on which greyhounds were raced at weekends. At the top of the Down the old Workhouse stood isolated and grim, no housing around it to soften its lines. In the Park the few isolated villas that had been built would look odd to our eyes, used to the continuous line of houses. So too would the sight of the servants bustling about, and the smell of horses from the stables behind the villas. But we would recognise some of the buildings we see today, and the remnant of the Spa. And much of the Park itself has stayed the same, perhaps more open, anarchic and scruffy today than in 1890, but recognisably similar.

6 The First World War

In the years before and after the First World War the Park was beautifully kept and well protected, a haven of shrubs and trees. In some ways it retained a flavour of its origins as a private garden, carefully controlled, where ordinary people were allowed on their best behaviour. It was well looked after because the Corporation had money to spend. Albert and Hilda Newcombe were children then and remember the Park well:

> *"We didn't destroy things, we were dead scared of the policemen. They had two park policemen up there all of the time. You couldn't do much damage because they had sticks - those long slender sticks like wands - and if ever they caught you they'd whack your hands and legs for a bit. We loved teasing them. They had to catch you and we used to run away, but sometimes you'd run into one of them because he'd be hiding behind the bushes round the corner. We used to call them Fatty and Skinny. 'Here comes Fatty! Here comes Skinny!' we'd shout. The Park was locked up at night, and there were big railings. Before locking up time they used to go round ringing the bell. When the lake froze in winter there was skating, but you had to pay to skate."*

Games were restricted, as Albert remembers:

> *"We used the park for sports occasionally. But the idea of sports for schools in those days was totally out of order. You went to school and you stuck at school. The only time we did go up to the Park was when our headmaster got permission. I think it was once a month, and we went up there to play Rounders on a bit of green. Some of the greens were enclosed. We thought that was a great privilege. The unfortunate part about it was our*

headmaster wouldn't allow you to hit the ball hard in case you knocked it into the pond!"

Did all this stop the children from enjoying themselves? Of course not – except on Sundays, when best clothes were worn and playing in the park was strictly banned! In particular there was the stream to play in, running all the way down the hill into the lake, or the pond as locals call it.

Queen's Park swan. "The pond was our favourite place ..."

Albert recalls that:

"The pond was a very favourite place, because in those days it was used quite a lot for kids' boats, lovely boats some of them had. They used to make these sailing boats, quite big ones, and bring them round on trolleys. I also remember little miniature steamboats. You'd see them sitting at the side with some paraffin in and they would take an hour to heat and get a bit of steam up to go across the lake. They used to go about 20 yards and stop, and of course you weren't allowed to get into the pond to rescue them."

...in the afternoons the children would bring their small wooden yachts...This one was found in the attic of a house in West Drive

June Marshall also recalls the activity around the pond:

"On Sunday mornings men would sail their big metal boats and in the afternoons the children would bring their small wooden yachts with white cotton sails. All the swans would gather on the island and flap and hiss at the boats. In the summer you'd see dozens and dozens of kids round there, tadpoling and catching newts. We used to go down and buy a long cane for a penny and then we'd go to Foots and buy a tadpole net and fix it on the end of this long cane so you could get it further out than the others, getting the newts and things. We would bring them home and then get chased

all round the place by our mother for putting them in the bowl on the washstand."

The park had it characters too. Hilda Newcombe remembers a Belgian refugee walking along the top of the park, lifting up all the ivy and filling a bucket with snails to eat:

" . . . because he was a Belgian and they love snails, don't foreigners?". There were also the itinerant photographers.

Albert recalls:

"We got caught there once - the old confidence trick. He saw all three of us playing in the park and said 'Let me take your picture'. Well he sat us down - I remember the spot even now where we were - I was squatting and Hilda and Cecil were standing on either side of me. I had one of those straw hats; we all wore hats, like the old sailors. He took our photograph and found out where we lived and came round with them a few days afterwards to our mother and made her buy them. We wouldn't have done it but that's how they caught you out in those days. They were on to a good racket, perhaps 'cos they thought we looked a bit respectable."

In 1914... new tennis courts. Photograph by Harry Avery who lived at no 1 West Drive

Small changes did occur even to the new Edwardian Park. In 1900 one of the two islands in the pond was removed, to make a larger expanse of open water. In 1909 the large Bowling Green was established, and in 1911 the first playground was built. In 1914 a croquet lawn and new tennis courts were constructed. In 1915 a suggestion originally thrown out at the opening ceremony was finally able to be acted upon. For years William Godley, a Brighton tradesman living in Montreal Road, had been pestered in the Park by children asking him the time. When he died in 1912 he left a bequest of £1,000 for the Clock Tower to be built.

Queen's Park Fountan constructed to celebrate the transfer of the park to Brighton Corporation and dedicated on 14 October 1893

7 Between the Wars

The First World War left no lasting scars on the Park, save the careful painting out of the word 'German' on the Spa portico, but after it the number of people using it grew rapidly. Its character began to change as Brighton grew around it, expanding up the hill in the direction of the race track and across towards Whitehawk. Around the fringes of the Park the remaining gaps were filled in as more villas were built in both East and West Drives. The area was still very sedate throughout the 1920s and 1930s.

June Marshall remembers:

> *"The Drives were very quiet, with hardly any traffic and an ideal spot to ride bikes. All the houses had servants. A horse and cart from Gigins at 'Bakers Bottom' (Craven Vale) delivered fresh bread daily. There was a funny little man with a donkey and cart who came round once a week with all the groceries. Daisy the Donkey wore a straw hat with her ears poking up through."*

June recalls the Park itself as a wonderful place between the Wars.

> *"The waterfall in the middle always gushed and water danced its way down across the gardens. Lupins about four feet high and of many different colours grew round the Bowling Green. There were masses of Syringa and Mock Orange blossom everywhere, the perfume was overpowering. There were Laburnum trees behind the swings, with yellow, hanging blossoms and we picked the pea-pods to play 'shops'. There were loads of conker trees to the southwest of the fountain. Girls used to make dolls' house furniture with them, using pins and cotton woven across the back. Boys soaked them in vinegar and baked them to play conkers. The big, pink fountain provided the*

most delicious cold water, and was a popular place for playing tag around. The little seat by the entrance to the swings was the 'courting' seat and couples used to sit and kiss as it was hidden back a bit. And then there were sweetheart leaves – those spotty laurel leaves the Victorians loved. You wrote the name of a boy you fancied on it and put it in your shoe. If it went black you would marry him."

Despite the vigilance of the Park Keepers the children still managed to get up to mischief. When the Keeper rang his warning bell (just before four o'clock in the winter and eight in the summer) they would hare for the gate by the lake at this was the last to close. But everyone – even Dick Braybon from one of the big houses – remembered climbing over the gates at least once to get out after the Park had closed. And some went further - Jack Parish and his friends managed to scale the Clock Tower after hours by hanging on to the copper lightning conductor!

The playground made a big difference for the children, as Jack Parish remembers:

"They made a proper lot of swings, which were good. With the babies' swings you used to have a wooden box arrangement on the seats with bits and pieces and you'd to lift the baby in and push the wooden bar back down into place again. There was no tarmac. All the equipment was in mud. If you went down the chute on a wet day you finished up in a great big puddle. There was a big chute and a small chute, for over-elevens at one end and under-elevens at the bottom end."

8 The Second World War

With the onset of the Second World War plans were laid in 1939 to build two air raid shelters in the Park. Initially these were to be brick structures above ground, but bad experience with these meant the shelters were eventually put underground, one at the southern end of the Clock Tower Green and the other next to the children's playground. They were filled in after the war but their outline can still be seen on the grass during dry summers. As part of the war effort most of the railings round the Park were cut down, as were the ornamental railings of the private gardens fronting the houses round the Drives. Denis Bignell remembers being paid nine pence for his garden railings in West Drive. Sometime during the war the top part of the stream was filled in, leaving only the last stretch through the Rest Garden, which still exists today.

The War produced all sorts of excitement. During the Blitz the German bombers took a line between the piers for their run-in to London. When such air raids were on many people used the cellars of Attree's Villa as additional shelter. David McCarthy used those shelters - just once. On that visit a person in clerical garb came round spraying everyone with insecticide. David's grandmother doughtily said

> *'If that is what they think of us we'll take our chances with the Germans at home'.*

June Marshall's family would set off as it was getting dark, with their blankets and gas mask tins, to go down into the cellars.

> *"There were wooden bunks and I remember often waking up to hear the Air Raid Wardens shouting at women who had brought soldiers in. I used to hate it. There were a sort of toilets at the end of each block and you could see people's feet at the bottom of the door".*

One morning in 1942 boys on the playground of the College in the Villa were machinegunned by a German aircraft and minor injuries sustained, though the worst injury was to the dignity of the Headmaster, Brother Aloysius, who had two boys land on top of him as everyone dived for cover. The following year June Marshall was at the top of the big slide in the playground just as a squadron of Flying Fortresses flew over, going home westwards.

"We were all looking up at them and two suddenly touched wings and bits came off. They seemed to float and there was this awful grinding noise. I was only about seven and just froze, and the Park Keeper raced up the steps, grabbed me and slid us both down the slide and into the bushes. I got all scratched. There were some awful, dull thumps and I believe some of the debris landed on the Race Hill."

The Park escaped any enemy bombing but bombs fell nearby, and one night an 'incendiary chandelier' lit up the whole of the northern end. Houses in Egremont Place and Upper Rock Gardens were destroyed where the new flats now stand. Possibly the target for these bombs was the Zylo ammunition works in Marine View.

At the outbreak of war, a number of dinghies had been brought from the beaches and tied up round the island, but with the frequent showers and leaks most of them finished up at the bottom of the lake. With the beaches closed people also bathed in the lake in hot weather. Summer 1943 saw the introduction of pleasure boating to keep the children's spirits up. In the months leading up to the invasion Denis Bignell remembers that many military vehicles were tested in a run through the lake to see if they were waterproof, always watched by small crowds. Canadian troops also practised bridge building and dismantling. About a week before D-Day all types of military vehicles took shelter under the trees, before moving off to ports along the coast to cross to France.

BRIGHTON : THE RESTRICTED ZONE

Brighton had been a restricted zone for much of the Second World War, with movement of people in and out of the area only by permission. But from spring 1944 the town was flooded with military men and equipment; Brighton became one huge armed camp. Troops were billeted on families, tanks lined most roads, supply dumps were piled in streets and garages were commandeered to service equipment.

Men with strange northern accents came too, to work on the ships and the roads - many street corners had to concreteted to minimise the damage from tank tracks turning. All roads leading back into Sussex were similarly crammed.

Suddenly, late on June 5th, all was quiet, the streets were empty. It felt like a ghost town. From early on the 6th it was the sky that held the attention as continuous waves of aircraft roared overhead. The invasion of Europe had begun.

9 Post War Park

The pond in Queen's Park in 1957

After the war the Park entered a new phase. Brighton itself was changing, with redevelopment taking place and living conditions improving. In the 1950s and 60s the Edward Street area was demolished, the road widened and new housing constructed. The summer bed-and-breakfast business still flourished, but social changes had begun which were to see the gradual decline of the holiday trade in Brighton. The Park and its surroundings were not as smart as they had been. Pennant Lodge, which had become first a convalescent and then nursing home in the 1960s, was abandoned. Queen's Park Hall next door became a furniture depository before being demolished, and Attree Villa, once the pride of the park, was abandoned and eventually pulled down in the early Seventies. Even the Spa, which had been producing bottled drinks for nearly a century and a half, fell into disuse after 1962.

The loss of its gates and railings made the park a very different place. Although they had lent the Park a slightly forbidding air, their removal made proper supervision nigh impossible. In the wake of complaints about damage to the Clock Tower and the bowling green the Corporation could only reply that it had no responsibility for the Park except 'during normal opening times'. Proposals to reinstate some form of railings after the war were turned down on grounds of cost. Instead limited lighting was provided and shrubs removed in an attempt to make the area safer and easier to police. The Park itself was like an ageing star, proud of its memories but somehow a little faded and worn. During the day many felt the place was overrun with dogs, and at night it was plain dangerous.

At this parlous juncture a new phase of the Park's history began. This time the architects of the Park's transformation were not the grandees of the racecourse or the Corporation but the local people.

The Royal Spa in its derelict state in 1967

In the 1970s it was campaigning by those who used the Park that pushed through changes that make the park what it is today.

The first of these concerned the Royal Spa. In 1967 Brighton Council decided to demolish it, but after a Public Enquiry it was listed, thus preventing demolition of much of the the exterior and in particular the gracious columns and arches that had formed the entry to the Pump Room. Sadly the Pump Room itself had already been vandalised beyond repair. In 1972 plans were lodged to develop the site as a casino and restaurant, which were fiercely contested by the local community who campaigned for the Spa to be developed into a nursery school. A new community newspaper, Queen Spark, became a major weapon in this fight. By 1974 the Corporation, now the Council, had accepted plans for a nursery school, but the fight wasn't over.

QueenSpark
The history of the Royal Spa
Royal Spa threatened

QueenSpark, first issue of the community newspaper in the early 1970s

Deterioration of the Spa continued, mostly due to vandalism. It wasn't until 1976, after the Park became part of a Conservation Area, that contracts were finally signed with a builder for the erection of the adjacent Nursery School building, which opened the following year. One of the happiest occasions in the Park was the Garden Party in July 1978 to crown this tremendous achievement by the local community. Sadly, the new school buildings were destroyed when vandals started a fire in 1985, but were soon rebuilt and declared even better than before.

A second campaign concerned the playground. In August 1975 a group of parents formed a registered charity to raise the money to build a sandpit. Thanks to the generous help of several firms and much hard work from the Committee the sandpit was finally opened in summer 1977.

Sue and Dave Baker recall:

> *"It was a whole community effort and, to our surprise, the Council allowed us to get on with it. People contributed what they could, running the Committee, looking after children, learning to drive dumper trucks, persuading local firms to donate the sand. Once a passing builder stood and gave advice, another rolled up his sleeves and laid*

beautiful rows of bricks as we mixed cement, but mostly it was done with minimal expertise and maximum enthusiasm by local families."

A third campaign involved dogs. Complaints about them fouling the children's play areas led residents to mount a 'Dogs' Mess in the Park' campaign. After much lobbying a tiny area was designated dog-free. A photograph was then published of parents from Queen's Park School, with all available offspring, crowded into this minute space - standing room only - with one small dog enjoying the freedom of the park. That gave birth to the 'flagging initiative', called Parks for People, in which straws and triangles of paper were used to mark every dog turd in the Park. The result was a sea of flags covering the entire park, a graphic illustration of the problem. Eventually it was agreed that half the Park was to be made dog-free and a Dog Warden was appointed.

For a while the Park was tranquil, but then came the worst shock of all. On the night of 16th October 1987 a hurricane swept across Southern England, destroying something like thirty million trees and doing untold damage to buildings. Queen's Park was right in its path. Simon Maxwell remembers noticing how warm and humid the air was the night before and then waking soon after midnight to the sound of a howling wind. Looking out of the window onto the park he described what he could see:

"Great elm trees a hundred feet high, swaying in the wind and then crashing to the ground, flattening cars along the Drive and blocking all the roads. When dawn broke the Park had lost a hundred mature trees. There was a fallen tree every 10 yards along West Drive and people stood with tears in their eyes. The branches were collected and burned on a huge bonfire below the Clock Tower; it was like a funeral pyre, and burned for weeks."

10 Wildlife

However since the hurricane dozens of new trees have been planted. Most have escaped the vandals and have grown to twenty or thirty feet in height, whilst in the Wildlife Area dozens of self-sown wych elm saplings have created a small copse. These trees have continued to provide a highly successful haven for a wide diversity of wildlife, which benefit from the sheltered southerly aspect, the pond and the absence of insecticides. The Park also has the advantage of being near areas of open download, with a green route from the Racehill.

The pond has always been a focus for wildlife. In July 2008 visitors were amazed to find a large bird hunting and preening itself on the island. Some mistook it for a stork and others a crane, but most recognised it as a heron. This bold, young bird stayed for a month, feeding mainly on water snails and other small creatures sheltering in the duckweed. Throughout 2007 a raft of duckweed had acted as midwife to new life in the pond by oxygenating the water, allowing extensive underwater beds of hornwort weed to grow from the mud and millions of pond creatures to flourish. Water boatmen, freshwater shrimps and caddis fly larvae are the most numerous, followed by pea mussels, damsel fly and dragonfly nymphs. Frogs breed in the stream.

Herring gull taking off from the pond

When the pond was last cleared in 2005 it was found to contain a thousand carp, descendants from fish introduced to the pond by unknown members of the public. Carp are bottom feeders, which in a shallow pond like Queen's Park seriously affect water quality by stirring up mud and uprooting the oxygenating weed. For this reason they were not replaced. Belligerent herring gulls have now displaced the smaller black-headed gulls who used to use the pond, and have also sadly driven away the wild mallards, coots and moorhens by persistent predation of their chicks.

Geese on the Queen's Park pond

A wide variety of birds is much in evidence throughout the Park. If one sits for a short while blackbirds, robins, wrens, dunnocks, blue tits and great tits are likely to appear. Jays, long tailed tits and greater spotted woodpeckers occasionally pass through, and in spring migrating whitethroats, redstarts, fire-crests, chiff-chaffs and willow warblers rest here before moving on. Chaffinch and greenfinch are well established in the Wildlife Area and the tinkling chatter of the once rare goldfinch is evident in the high bushes and trees by the tennis courts. Song thrush and mistle thrush maintain only a fragile hold due to grey squirrel predation. Twice in recent years a sparrow hawk has taken up station for a few weeks in the high beeches by the cascade, and from time to time one of the local peregrine falcons is seen, circling high in the sky scanning for prey.

On summer evenings swifts skim the pond catching flies for their young waiting in the eaves of the houses around Queen's Park. At dusk and dawn pipistrelle bats hunt the same quarry with flickering wings and aerobatic dexterity. Both swift and pipistrelle numbers have declined by over half in the last quarter of a century, so to help combat that bird and bat roosting boxes have been installed in the Clock Tower.

Spring 2008 saw the first flowering of the new wildflower meadow, initiated by City Parks gardeners using a wildflower seed mix plus over one thousand individual plants. It will take six years to reach maturity but already by any June this bank by the southernmost tennis court is dotted with yellow rattle, ox eye daisy, hawkbit, ragged robin, red campion, poppy, mullen and mallow. In July comes self-heal, ladies bedstraw, knapweed, fennel, bird's foot trefoil, spear thistle and corn cockle, and in August wild marjoram, harebell and evening primrose. On sunny days it buzzes with insect life and it is hoped that the Blues and other butterflies typical of chalk grassland will eventually breed there.

Like the human visitors the living creatures that every day share the Park have also changed, with new species becoming established whilst others have been lost. Butterflies such as speckled wood, comma, peacock and red admiral now patrol the shady paths and sunny spaces of the Wildlife Area. In the last twenty years the problem of grey squirrels and their predatory behaviour has caused concern because of their very high density of over four per hectare in the Park. The more acceptable hedgehog continues to forage through the night hours and in the hour before dawn foxes patrol the Park's open spaces, whilst badgers trundle up its grassy slopes.

Plans for the further development of the habitat are being made, with an improved system of paths and the addition of more plants and trees characteristic of the Downs and the Wealden woodlands in order to broaden the diversity of species which can once again

The opening of the Park 1892

Yacht race on the pond in the Park

11 People and Park

Humans as well as the wildlife need to be considered in planning the Park. It has always been a focus for sport, ranging from the casual kick-about to the frisbee fanatics. Some of the games are more formally located. There has been a tennis club in Queen's Park for over eighty years, being one of the founder clubs of the Brighton Parks Tennis Association. The handwritten record book shows that there were 71 members in 1939 and the club made a profit of £5.5s.1d. Some of the club trophies date back to the early fifties. Originally there were grass courts, later shale courts and nowadays hard courts. The clubhouse was initially shared with the bowlers, whose club also dated from the 1930s, but with the demise of the bowling green due to persistent vandalism the tennis members now have sole use of it. The Club continues to thrive and passers-by can see competitive tennis most evenings and at weekends. Overlooking the courts there is a bench dedicated to Brenda Jewell. Brenda was treasurer and secretary for over 50 years and could often be seen walking to the Club with her Scottie dogs.

But the heart of the Park has always been the children, and even today ten year olds still appreciate the place in their unique way.

> *"My favourite part is where the Clock Tower is because there's lots of room to play in the field. Sometimes when I go there with my friends we enjoy making up stories about the Clock Tower, like there's a minotaur in there waiting to eat us because it's so scary... We had to do a cross country round the park every Monday and Wednesday. It was really fun... there are lots of places to play football in the football season and cricket in the cricket season... The café is nice and friendly... when we go to the Park in the summertime there is an enormous queue for the café and we have to*

wait and wait for an ice cream... I love the playground. I once spent an hour on the swings. I was nearly sick... I think the pond is great, and I hope it stays clean. Sometimes I find the Park a bit boring in the winter... There is an overhanging rock just above the place where the water from the Secret Garden gushes down into the pond. If you let yourself very slowly down it until you are three quarters of the way down you find a small ledge. I can remember falling off that ledge into the stream and thinking I was drowning... Queen's Park has always been a

Postcard depicting the pond at Queen's Park. The carefully positioned winding paths was typical of park design of the late 19th century

12 Attree Villa

Having traced the story of the Park from when it was only a gleam in John Armstrong's eye in 1822 through to today when it is a jewel amongst local public parks, in order to complete the picture we also need to look at the buildings associated with it. Indeed it is difficult to think of the Park in isolation, for those buildings have always had a symbiotic relationship with it. For most of its history Queen's Park was graced by several stately structures, of which only vestiges remain. It gained a modestly palatial atmosphere from the imposing Italianate Villa at the north end and the elegance of the neo-classical Spa at the south, an atmosphere that still clings to it today.

In late 1829 Thomas Attree commissioned Charles Barry to design him a villa and accompanying gardens overlooking what was then called 'Brighton Park'. Barry is best known as the joint architect of the Houses of Parliament, but he spent much of his early career working on buildings in Brighton, designing most of the Gothic Revival Parish Church of St Peter's and the Sussex County Hospital. The villa he built for Attree was something of a landmark in British architectural history, for it introduced a new phase of Italianate quattrocento architecture into the country - the result of several stays in Italy in Barry's youth. Perhaps even more important for Queen's Park the setting of the villa within parkland was an essential, core part of the design. Barry's idea was to surround his buildings with fine formal, architectural gardens and then gradually harmonise the setting into the natural parkland beyond.

To the ordinary observer it was the gardens that wafted the warm breezes and al fresco living of Italy into Queen's Park. Ingeniously laid out on varying levels connected by balustraded terraces and sprinkled with statuary they were a stark contrast to the usual post-

The gazebo or belvedere once part of the Italian terraced garden of Attree Villa

Regency garden. On the south side of the villa the gardens were sunk below the level of the forecourt. On the opposite side of the house the orchard was sunk below the garden. Miniature 'mountain ranges' were planted with trees. Even today, under the bleak seventies housing, these abrupt changes in ground level are still very evident. The graceful gazebo or belvedere, which now stands so oddly in the midst of modern blocks of flats, used to hold a marble statue of the Emperor Aurelius. A double flight of stone steps led down into the orchard; the piers at the top (still in evidence) were adorned with figures of dogs. There were also 'well arranged and highly ornamental' flower and vegetable gardens, melon and cucumber pits, and grape and peach houses.

These gardens significantly helped to make Barry's career, for their design attracted the attention of the Duke of Sutherland, one of the richest men in the country, and persuaded him to commission Barry to do similar work at the Duke's Staffordshire seat, and later at his many other houses in London, around England and in Scotland.

When Duddell moved in after Attree's death he renamed it Duddell Villa, but he failed to look after the property. When it was auctioned in 1887 the papers contain a sad commentary on Duddell's impact on the place by Somers Clarke Junior: "Attree Villa fell into the hands of one quite unable to appreciate its beauties and of those surrounding gardens, which suffered grievously. The terrace walls were covered with mounds of turf and the whole thing much defaced. Mr Attree was my father's partner and many happy hours have I spent as a child playing upon the pretty terraces, now much altered".

Nevertheless the sale particulars for the house boasted of "Three attics on the upper floor, Four bedrooms on the Chamber Floor with a bathroom containing a wc with lift up lavatory basin, On the

Ground Floor an Entrance Hall with handsome staircase, Dining Room and Drawing Room with casement windows opening onto the terrace and a frieze around the ceiling in bas-relief representing the Siege of Troy, a Billiard Room, Conservatory and Library. There is a large basement for the servants and six large arches for wine cellars. Outside are Four-stall Stables, a Laundry, Coal House and Dung Pit plus Glasshouses and Forcing Houses". Despite this grandiloquence Duddell Villa with its five acres of grounds failed to elicit the necessary bid and soon stood vacant. Plans for a zoo were mooted but never got off the ground.

One person connected with the Villa at this time was Duddell's son by Kate, William Du Bois Duddell, who had a distinguished career as an electrical engineer, inventing the oscilloscope and the singing arc among numerous other scientific instruments. Exhibiting the arc to a Learned Society in London he was able to make it 'play' God Save the King. Nevertheless both the oscilloscope and the arc had very important applications, the one in radio and the other in wireless telegraphy. William is buried in Brighton.

After the very louche life of Duddell one might think the next owner of the Villa would be a comparatively grey figure. But you would be wrong, for enter the mad Cardinal. Though only occupying the Villa for a short time before his death Edward Henry Howard, the uncle of the Duke of Norfolk, must have been a strange figure in Queen's Park. Howard became a Catholic priest after a short spell in the British Army, rising to Archbishop, Cardinal and Protector of the English College in Rome. The Italian atmosphere of the Villa and gardens would have made his time there seem as if he was back in the land where he had spent most of his life, especially as he brought with him six servants and an Italian valet. He is buried in Arundel. The 1891 census describes him bluntly as a Lunatic.

The Xaverian College, In 1966 the De La Salle brothers moved their school to the former Convent of the Sacred Heart Upper Drive, Hove

The Villa later became the Sons of Temperance Convalescent Home until 1909 when the Xaverian Order took it over for a boy's school This school had originally started as an orphanage run by Flemish and Dutch brothers in Mayfield, Sussex, during the 1870s but gradually developed into a high-class College for both day and boarding pupils. The opening of the College was a big affair, with the Bishop of Southwark saying Mass and blessing the chapel and grounds in front of a large attendance by local residents.

Before the College opened considerable work was done on the Villa. The stable block and gardener's lodge were turned into classrooms, and inside the Villa the Greek panels in the Drawing Room of designs from the Iliad were painted out as unsuitable for the chapel of a boys' school!

However old Xaverians recalling the school say they scarcely set foot in the Villa, which was the Brothers' residence, except to serve at early Mass in the chapel or receive a caning for misdemeanours such as bad marks in Latin, passing notes or making water bombs in class. The main school building was some

100 yards away, a rather drab L-shaped affair overlooking a tiled courtyard, with access to the upper floor by iron steps. The Preparatory classes were housed separately, on the site of the former stables. Xaverians came in for a tough time from the children at the local Schools. One Old Boy remembers having to run the gauntlet of the 'Hendon Street Gang' from St Luke's:

Race at the Xaverian College school. Note the balustrade surrounding the terracing of the Italian garden

> *"There was a lot of hostility... 'College Cads' was the usual term. Their greatest delight was to snatch your cap off and throw it over the road, take your satchel and empty the books into the pond... I was terrified of them... We used to call them the Elementaries... If there'd been snow then they'd come and invade the school just at the time we were coming out and set upon us with lumps of ice."*

There were running battles between the College and pupils from Queen's Park School at the school entrance, with both sides hurling any missiles that came to hand at each other. The Xaverian boys by no means took the invasions lying down.

Due to dwindling numbers in their order, the Xaverian Brothers sold the College in 1960 to the De La Salle Order, but the newcomers would be at the helm for only six years before moving to Hove. The Villa was acquired by a firm of developers and very soon was in an advanced state of dilapidation.

It was repeatedly vandalised, including the chapel with its organ and stained glass windows, and lead was stolen from the roof. Ownership passed to a new company, Seavista Ltd. In 1968 it was placed under a Preservation Order and given a Grade II* listing yet, as it was so full of rot and would have cost around £150,000 to save, it was finally demolished in the Seventies despite many protests. All that remains of this fine structure and setting are the forlorn gazebo, a few pillars (including one at the former drive

The Pepperpot or Pepperbox

13 Pepperpot

An underground passageway led from the stable yard of Attree Villa to the circular Italianate tower we all know today as the Pepperpot or Pepperbox. Barry's designs show that at one stage he was considering crowning the tower with an onion dome, under the influence of Nash's remodelled Pavilion. The Pepperpot stands 60 feet above the level of the Park, with the top of the cupola 200 feet above sea level. There has long been speculation about its purpose, ranging from claims that it was no more than an elaborately disguised sewer vent to suggestions that it was intended as an observation tower. It was in fact almost certainly designed to house a horizontal wind wheel for raising water for the Villa (and possibly the whole estate). It soon became obsolete, a permanent water supply being obtained from the Water Company using their newly built reservoirs nearby.

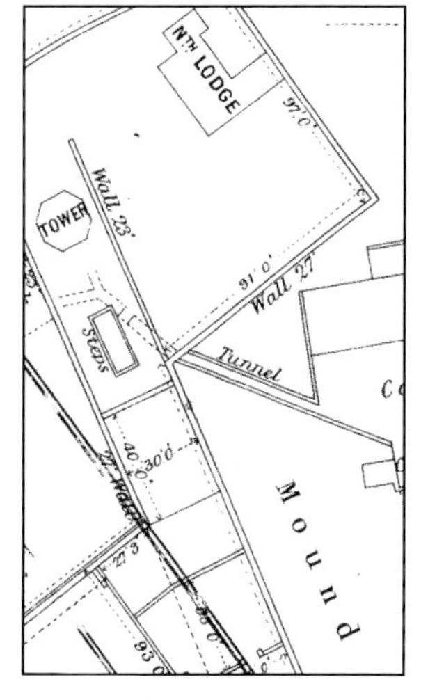

The 1863 plan shows the tunnel (above 'Mound') which connected the Pepperpot with Mr Duddell's villa

Since then the Pepperpot has seen a variety of uses. Before it passed into the hands of the Corporation George Duddell had designated it as the Tower Press and used it to print his halfpenny paper, the 'Brighton Mail'. In 1892 at the Park opening the Mayor thought 'there was no tower in England that gave a more extensive and varied view of both land and sea... Not only was it useful and ornamental but it would probably bring in a small revenue.' Since then the Pepperpot has been used as a war-time observation tower, a meeting place for youth groups, an artist's studio and even a public toilet.

Sadly the Pepperpot is now empty, neglected and falling into disrepair.

German Spa and Pump Room, aquatint by M U Sears circa 1835

BRIGHTON PARK.

MR. ARMSTRONG, the projector and proprietor of the Park, begs leave respectfully to acquaint the Nobility, Gentry, and the Public, that it is now open for admission, (Sundays excepted.) The celebrity which Brighton has acquired by the presence of Royalty, and the salubrity of the air, induced the proprietor to direct his attention to the formation of a Park, for public resort: conceiving it would form a novel and desirable addition to the various sources of amusement. Under that impression, between sixty and seventy acres have been so converted, at a considerable expence, lying to the north of the Marine-parade, and opening to the downs by a carriage-drive and promenade, forty feet wide, and nearly a mile and a half long; including an interesting valley, interspersed with plantations and ornamental groups of trees, surmounted by allotments surrounding the whole, for the erection of detached villas, which will command an uninterrupted view of the varied scenery of the Park, the downs, and the sea. Just within the eastern entrance is an elegant PUMP-ROOM, intended for the supply of the celebrated MINERAL WATERS OF GERMANY, which adds a striking feature to the general effect.

His Majesty having been graciously pleased to signify his approbation of the design, and several of the nobility and gentry, who have seen the Park, having expressed great satisfaction, and promised to sanction the undertaking, it is anxiously hoped, when the improvements, which are in progress, are completed, that it will be thought worthy of public patronage.

TERMS AND CONDITIONS.

A Ticket for a Family for		Twelve Months	.. Two Guineas.
A ditto	ditto	Three Months	.... One Guinea.
A ditto	ditto	One Month	.... Half-a Guinea.
A ditto	One Person	Twelve Months	.... One Guinea.
A ditto	ditto	Three Months	.... Half-a-Guinea.
A ditto	ditto	One Month	.... Five Shillings;

Every Non-Subscriber to pay Three-pence each time of admission.

No lodger to be included in a family ticket.—No dogs admitted, nor servants exercising their masters' horses.

Subscriptions will be received at the Banks and Libraries; and also at the Cottage, in the Park

A newspaper advertisement publicising the "salubrity of the air" in Brighton Park—as it was then known

14 German Spa

At the opposite end of the Park was the Spa. In 1824 Friederich Struve must have looked at his new Manufactory with pleasure. The German Spa, soon to be the Royal German Spa, was a graceful addition to John Amstrong's proposed park. Though a stranger in the land he had high hopes for his spa waters with all the aristocratic clientele in nearby Brighton. Struve was born in Saxony in 1781 and trained as a doctor at no less than three Universities in Germany and Austria. After a short spell as a doctor in his home town he moved to Dresden to work as a research chemist, one of the very earliest of that profession. An accidental explosion in his laboratory left him partially crippled, and touring the many spas of Germany in the hope that their waters might restore him to health - which they did to some degree - he found the long journeys between them desperately tiresome. The idea came to him of manufacturing the waters so that patients could avoid such journeys over the awful roads of the time. Back in his laboratory he discovered how to do it. Struve's achievement is really two separate achievements, and the second and less well-known one was the more important for him financially, and for his successors.

An alcove in the wall of the Spa

Struve discovered that if carbonic acid is diluted in plain water and mineralised rock is dropped in it and then subjected to high pressure the water leaches out the mineral in the rock and the resulting fluid is indistinguishable from the spa waters that people travelled so far to imbibe. Struve carefully analysed the rocks around the springs of the spas, for instance the basalt around Marienbad, the felspar around Tieplitz and the granular rock around Eiger, and found that by using such rock he could produce the waters of these famous spas. However there was a second problem. It was well-known that bottling these spa waters was not a useful practice because the bottled water rapidly lost its crucial characteristics. Struve found that if the 'spa' water was bottled at high pressure into a bottle that already contained some carbonic acid gas then it could be sealed and sent all over the world without losing any of its value. This was to be the more valuable achievement for him financially, and for his successors.

One of the many Hooper Struve bottles found buried in the vicinity of the Park (see the lettering around the base)

Struve had taken as his partner an Englishman who was working in Dresden, and with him had set up his Manufactories all over Europe, as far afield as Berlin, Warsaw, Kiev. Moscow and St Petersburg. Turning his eyes to England and arriving here in 1823 it seemed that Brighton was the right place for the venture, no doubt advised by his partner Swaine, but there was both opposition and distrust to be overcome. The opposition was from the owners of the other Spas of England, and the Wick chalybeate spring in Hove in particular, who saw their business disappearing. The distrust was because of the novelty of the process. Struve and Swaine also had to take into account the social side of 'taking the waters', which in places like Tunbridge Wells or Cheltenham almost took precedence over the health-giving aspects. However Struve was first and foremost a medical man, and saw himself as dispensing a medicine, not an excuse for a ball or a rout. So the partners looked around for a discreet location, away from the Steine and its jollifications and high land prices, but sufficiently close and housed in a building of sufficient elegance to attract the right sort of patron.

John Armstrong's prospective park seemed ideal. There were the beginnings of gardens, it was near the road along the cliff tops and on the edge of the town as it then was. Armstrong was also likely to be very much in need of the money from the lease of the plot, but he also insisted that the building should enhance the park. The lease lays down that a 'Manufactory' for the preparation of 'factitious' waters was to be built on the land and that it was to face north into the park and be hidden behind a 'Colonnade or

Ornamental front'. That colonnade is all that is left today. A well was to be dug and ornamental trees and shrubs planted. The original bill from the builders, Messrs Cooper and Lynn, is still in the Brighton Library.

A paragraph in the Brighton Gazette's 'Fashionable Chronicle', nine months after the Spa opened, provides a striking description of it. "The building consists of a large, handsome room fifty or sixty feet in length and of proportionate breadth and height. A fine flight of steps leads to the noble saloon, on which are placed Ionic columns, supporting a portico in the purest Grecian taste. On the side of the Saloon opposite the entrance runs a counter, behind which are ranged the cocks that supply fifteen different kinds of waters. The high ceiling is bordered by and centred with a two-tier wreath of acanthus leaves around a temptingly large and realistic bunch of grapes". The front of the Pump Room was two thirds glass. From Cooper and Lynn's account light colours such as lilac and grey were used for decoration, with opal on the ceiling and plaster mouldings picked out in gold. The floor was in polished oak, the doors and the majestic serving counter in mahogany.

Ceiling boss from the Spa. If a chandelier hung from the centre of the ceiling, as seems likely, it must have been removed when the room was turned into a ginger beer brewery in the 1900s. Hooper Struve were the pre-eminent brewers of ginger beer in the country in the first part of the 20th century

The range of ailments that the waters were said to help with, or even cure, was wide-ranging, but most of them concerned digestive problems. Since one aim of the waters was to purge the system a range of toilets for immediate use was also provided. That meant that a reasonably well-functioning sewer system was needed, since the 'Top Ten' of the aristocracy would not come if the place stank. A very large cesspit was dug and double sewerage connections made to ensure that the bodily functions could be completed with grace and in comfort.

Before he opened Struve naturally sought to patent his system to protect himself from imitators. However he had to be careful. The simple notion of adding salts to water and peddling them as Seltzer

Water had been carried on since the late eighteenth century, when Jacob Schweppe started the practice in Switzerland. Schweppe had even opened his own Manufactory in London before Struve arrived. Hence Struve patented his pressure equipment, which was the heart of his process. He was also distinguished from Schweppe by his emphasis on the medicinal qualities of his waters as opposed to simple table waters.

Struve's insistence that he dispensed a medicine led him to inveigh against those of his clientele who insisted on trying several waters in a single visit, on the principle that the more the better. He had done a lot work on the effects of the different waters, and his advertising was very careful to distinguish complaint and appropriate water. Struve took strong objection to multiple sampling; it was not a case of pick and mix. His view of himself also meant that the Pump Room was open only in the mornings, to allow the aristocracy to prepare their systems for another evening of excess elsewhere.

Entrance arches to Queen's Park from Egremont Place.

In its Regency and Georgian heyday the German Spa attracted a huge clientele. It was said that on a typical day the chalk track up to the Spa from the cliff-top road had over a hundred carriages waiting for their owners. In 1826 Canning visited the Spa, the year before he was made Prime Minister. It also attracted a Royal Warrant for the sale of its curative waters and the patronage of many of the upper class visitors to Brighton. Struve's waters were delivered to the Royal Pavilion and to Windsor Palace for the benefit of a sick King, but it seems Royalty never actually visited the Royal Spa .

Struve died in 1840, and he is well remembered in his home country. Struvestrasse is a major street in Dresden.

At the Spa the factory entrance and yard was through a gate in what is now Park Street, but was then called Spa Hill. Water - the source of all the activity - continued to be drawn up by steam pump from the well originally sunk by Struve in the 1820s, the depth of which was about 150 feet. It was also questionably claimed to be delivered to the Company's even larger factory near Tottenham Court Road in London. Waters from both factories were put in bottles with labels stating 'Manufactured from the waters of the Renowned Spring of the Royal German Spa, Brighton'.

From the start Struve's waters were bottled. A one pint bottle of Marienbad water in 1840 cost 8 old pence (about £1.50 nowadays). This bottling became central to the business. The character of Brighton as a home of elegance slowly changed and by the middle of the nineteenth century the Spa attracted fewer and fewer customers. A contemporary observer at that time said the Pavilion had become a 'cage for mice and spiders and the Pump Room fallen away', and by 1886 the 'Brighton Almanac' could note "The once fashionable method of drinking waters by persons going to the Royal German Spa is a thing of the past". In the face of this challenge the factory business was built up on the strength of the widespread sale of bottled waters to hotels and boarding houses (and eventually to shops) in the Brighton area. The excellence of them, combined with their Royal Warrant, spawned imitations. By

Photograph by Chris Lowe. A young heron on Queen's Park pond, produced for 'The Story of Queen's Park'

Photograph by Chris Lowe. A group of ox-eye daisies in the wildflower meadow in Queen's Park, produced for 'The Story of Queen's Park'

the middle of the century at least two chemists in London were also manufacturing 'Brighton Seltzers' – artificial mineral waters rivalling the quality and fame of the Queen's Park 'originals'. One of these imitators was William Hooper, who ran a substantial chemical business in London.

By this time the Struve factory in the Spa was producing a whole variety of bottled fizzy drinks, including lemonade and ginger beer. These popular drinks were fast outselling the traditional German mineral waters, feeding a market among the pubs and corner shops of a rapidly expanding town, very different from the aristocratic customers of earlier times. In 1891 the Struve Company merged with the Hooper Company and the new organisation concentrated on the production of ginger beer, lemonade and soda water, whilst still maintaining the prestigious lines. Genuine Brighton Seltzer continued to enjoy royal approval until the reign of George VI. Bottles delivered to royalty at the Court of St James were individually wrapped in linen and delivered in hampers.

In the difficult years following the First World War the directors of the firm resolutely established new buildings - one brought in was an old aeroplane hanger - and installed new machinery at Queen's Park, thus enabling the Brighton company to continue through the 1920s. The title 'soft drinks' replaced 'mineral waters'. The firm was now first and foremost a busy and flourishing lemonade factory, a major player on the national soft drinks scene. It continued to be so for another 30 years under the management of Arthur West. His devotion to the firm became something of a legend. He and his family reoccupied the living quarters above the factory at the Spa, and for the first time in many years re-cultivated the garden where Regency patrons had first sauntered. The West's even adopted a pair of peacocks that had strayed away from the care of the Parks Department.

The 1930s were probably the years of greatest prosperity for the Brighton factory. But in 1940 the War Department commandeered the building and, for the first time in over 115 years, the Royal Spa closed its doors. A Gas Mask Issuing Station was set up in the Pump Room and above it a fire watching station was established. 'Soft Drinks Producing Unit No SE23' however continued limited manufacture under strict government regulations, but was finally closed 'for the duration' in 1943. After the war, business picked up quickly again but the very fact of increased demand and output made new, more up-to-date premises essential. The lease of the Royal Spa from Brighton Corporation was due to expire in 1962. In 1963 Hooper Struve moved to Lower Bevendean. The company was later taken over by conglomerates and has now lost its identity, though the Royal Warrant still remains today, but in the hands of Canada Dry (UK) Ltd.

Hooper Struve delivery lorry, date and place unknown

The Royal German Spa building remained the property of Hooper Struve and was used as a storage shed. Little effort was made by the firm, Brighton Council or local residents to preserve the elegant Regency Pump Room. Cut-glass partitions and mirrors, mahogany serving hatches, gilded mouldings – all were left to the mercy of the winds blowing in through cracks and broken panes and of the tramps who sought shelter there. Campaigning in the 1970s managed to preserve the neo-classical façade with its six fluted columns - only a shell, but at least a pleasing shell.

15 Other Buildings

The houses around the fringe of the Park were built over a wide spread of time and in varying styles. None of those from the earliest period, of the 1820s and 1830s, survive today. The majority of those in West Drive are Edwardian, but one of the earlier ones is still standing, namely Pennant Lodge, now called Queen's Park Villa, a very large, white building standing well back from the roadway in the north west corner. This was built around 1845, on the site of an even earlier 1830s house. Sale particulars from the 1860s describe the Villa as "having sloping lawns, garden, greenhouse, stabling, coach house and coachman's lodge...let on a lease at £204 p.a.'.

The house takes its name from the first owner, a Lady Pennant from a North Wales family with conspicuous relatives on both sides, namely the Spencer-Churchills and the Earls of Cardigan. Lady Pennant lived there only a short time around 1845 before it passed to Charles Freshfield, who gave his name to the nearby streets of that name. Freshfield was solicitor to the Bank of England and Member of Parliament for the City of London, and he leased the house through the 1850s and into the 1860s. The next known tenant was a landscape painter, Marmaduke Langdale and family, at the beginning of the twentieth century. After another gap, in 1927 Bernard Baron, the owner of the huge tobacco company Carreras Ltd, set up a convalescent home for his employees. When he died in 1929 his will decreed that it should continue to be used for 'sick people engaged in domestic, manual and clerical labour, with preference given to employees of Carreras Ltd'. In 1985 the house was refurbished and turned into offices.

Another early addition to the villas was Home Villa, now no 18 West Drive, built in the early 1880s. For most of the 1880s and 1890s a Reverend MacDonald lived there with his family and a mysterious Miss Butler. MacDonald was the chaplain to the Albion Hill Home for Penitent Women, or unmarried mothers, in Finsbury Road. Unlike the houses of the earlier part of the nineteenth century it has a steeply pitched roof, which sets it apart from them.

Pennant Lodge and Queen's Park Hall, earlier known as the New Villa

GEORGE BERESFORD

Beresford originally trained as an engineer, and spent some time in his early twenties working in that profession in India. However in 1888 he returned to England and changed course, attending the Slade School of Art.

He set up a photographic studio in Knightsbridge and became highly successful. In addition to Woolf he photographed Sir James Barrie, Keir Hardy, Herbert Asquith, Lloyd George, W B Yeats, Nancy Astor and Jacob Epstein among others. Nearly 200 of his portraits are held in the National Portrait Gallery.

Beresford was very interested in social reform and was an active member of the Fabian Society. In previous years he strongly supported the emancipation of women, and during World War One he donated all the profits from his business to the Red Cross as a gesture of opposition to the War.

Beresford lived in no 21 throughout the twenties and thirties. As Duddell before him he kept a menage. Little is known of Jessie Wilson, the mother of his sons, and even her surname is suspect. One of her sons claimed that Beresford took the name from Wilson Avenue.

Later the house became a nursing home, but the butler's room and servants quarters could still be identified. Staff at the Nursing Home said that occasionally women who had been at the Albion Hill Home would visit the house in West Drive and relate their memories. It is now a private home again. A third early house was Queen's Park Hall, sometimes called New Villa, also built in the 1880s, which sat alongside Pennant Lodge but is now under the row of houses lining Tower Road. For many years it was the home of the Reverend Scott and daughters who ran a School for Young Ladies there.

Just along the road from Home Villa is no 21 West Drive, put up in 1895 and for many years the home of George Charles Beresford. Born in Cheltenham in 1864 he went to the United Services College in Westward Ho in Devon where he met Rudyard Kipling, who subsequently wrote 'Stalky & Co.' based on their schoolday experiences. Beresford appears in the book as M'Turk. He set up as a portrait photographer and most of the great and good in politics and the arts sat for him between 1902 and 1930. Some of his photos, such as that of Virginia Wolf, are regarded as the iconic photographs of the subject. Beresford lived with Jessie Wilson, by whom he had two sons. After Beresford died the Wilson brothers ran a gravel business from the house. One of them remembered Kipling coming to no 21 and pointing out on a globe in the living room the places to which he had travelled.

Many of the Edwardian houses were designed by Thomas Buckwell, who had an architect's practice in North Street, Brighton. Buckwell's father was a local ship builder and timber merchant and Thomas had grown up in Egremont Place. He built nos 1 to 4 West Drive, and on retirement he moved with his family into another of his houses at no 6 West Drive.

West Drive, on the corner of Albion Hill, showing typical Buckwell houses

In this range of Buckwell houses, no 1 was owned by Harry Avery for many years. Brighton residents will remember his photographic shop in St James's Street, which was the most important such shop in the town right up to the 1960s. Avery had a garage and workshop built at the side of the house where he made concrete figures of monkeys and other animals, and these were set out in the front garden three sitting round a table. A concrete cat and dog sat on a wall. The local children would look out for them when passing by and the house became known by them as 'the monkey house'.

No 3 West Drive was owned by Thomas Gasson, a Cask & Timber merchant with a business off Edward Street. Whilst many of the houses around the Park sported fine stained glass windows, in this house they were particularly fine, being illustrative of 'Music and Plenty'. Next door, at no 4, William Towner lived in the 1900s. He was the son of a local baker and had started as a young printer on the 'Brighton Gazette' but finished up as the senior manager and the publisher of the Brighton Directories. The business became the Southern Publishing Company and is now Newsquest, publisher of the 'Argus'.

Further along at no 17 lived Mrs Ginnett, whose husband was the proprietor of a Circus. The house only dates from the 1930s and it has been claimed that the design of it was based on that of a doll's house owned by Princess Elizabeth. There is certainly a faint look of a doll's house about it. No 29 West Drive was also built by Beresford and is more decorated than others of his designs. It was lived in by Madame Bessie Basinet.

Moving round to East Drive we find that most of the houses were built a little later than those in West Drive and have more decoration. No 22 East Drive, also known as Haydon Lodge, was built in 1908 to designs by A J Hopkins of London with an original valuation of £1950. Although the design does share some features with other nearby Edwardian houses, namely the use of warm red brick and hung tiles, it also has some distinctive features. In particular there is a prominent glazed turret with a conical tiled roof and weather vane which enjoys panoramic views over the adjacent Park to the city and coast beyond, and as a consequence the house is locally referred to as 'the Tower House'. It was built by Archibald Trace as a speculation and initially occupied by a

Catherine Sykes, and then by an Augustus White, but in 1926 John Lloyd opened a school in the premises with the grand title of Queen's Park High, with Mrs Lloyd as the Principal. More recently it was occupied by Norbert Lynton who was Professor of the History of Art at the University of Sussex. After a brief incursion of squatters in 1986 the house is again in private occupation. Substantial damage was done to the turret in the hurricane of October 1987 but the weather vane remained steadfastly upright and still functions today, 100 years after installation.

NORBERT LYNTON

Norbert Lynton was born in Berlin in 1927 to a mixed Jewish Catholic family who fled the Nazis and came to England in the thirties. He taught art history in several academic institutions and at one time was the director of exhibitions for the Arts Council, mounting major shows at the Hayward Gallery. Lynton championed Modernism and was an early proponent of painters such as Pollock and Rothko amongst others.

He was primarily interested in the visual aspect of painting rather than the social or philosophical - clearly demonstrated in his last exhibition, put on at Brighton Museum in 2008, under the title 'Paintings Unwrapped'.

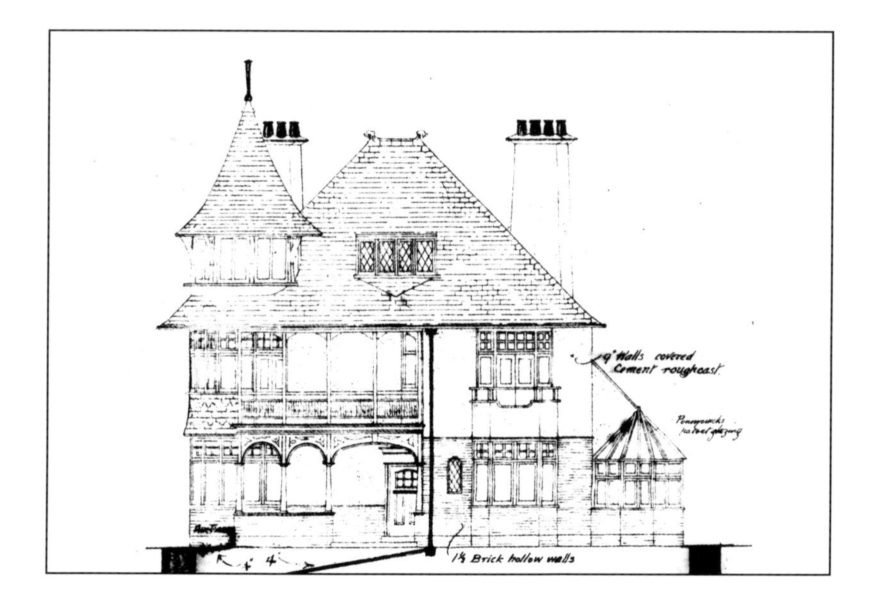

Haydon Lodge 22 East Drive

Joseph Sattin built a number of the houses in East Drive, and lived in one himself when he retired. No 23 East Drive was built in 1923 on the playground of the Lloyd school next door. In that year it was the 'Daily Mail' Show House of the Year. Once owned by the Chief Constable of the town it was later in the hands of a Mr McCabe, a jeweller with a business in Hatton Garden in London.

Tower Lodge beside the Pepper Pot and across from St Lukes church

In addition to the private villas there used to be the much older entrance lodges, dating from the park's earliest days. There were two of these. Egremont Lodge was at the south end of West Drive, adjacent to the elegant gateway. It is long gone, but in 1894 Albert Howell, the Corporation gardener, lived there. It is now an area of shrubbery. Up at the north end of the grounds, at the top end of Tower Road and in the shadow of the Pepperpot, was the Tower Lodge, now only a lawn in front of a block of flats.

In the grounds of the Attree Villa there was also the Gardener's Cottage, also known as North Lodge, hard on Queen's Park Terrace. In earlier years relatives of Duddell had lived in this cottage, including his favourite - though unacknowledged - son Frederick Vernon, who had brought up his family there. By 1890 Duddell's old Head Gardener, a Scot named James Spottiswood, lived there with his wife and four sons. In the 'Gardener's Magazine' of 1892 an article stated that Spottiswood was an able gardener, growing an astonishing variety of fine fruit in difficult conditions on the chalk. It listed the many varieties of apples and pears that were grown, and in particular the Beurre Claireau Pear of which there was a photograph of a tree laden with fruit.

FINE FRUIT

Among the variety of fine fruit at the Duddell's Villa were:

Pears: Beurre Superfine, Beurre Hardy, Beurre Diel, Beurre d'Amanlis, Doyenne du Comice, Brockworth Park, Louise Bonne of Jersey, Duchesse d'Angoulême.

Dessert apples: Cox's Orange Pippin, Ribston Pippin, King of the Pippins, Adams's Pearmain, Irish Peach, White Transparent, Lord Burghley, Margil, Kerry Pippin, Fearn's Pippin.

Kitchen apples: Lord Suffield, Ecklinville, Stirling Castle, Warner's King, Cobham, Allen's Everlasting, Yorkshire Greening, Cox's Pomona and Blenheim Pippin

16 Endpiece

Queen's Park has come a long way since its first beginnings. First it was a private pleasure garden, then a carefully tended municipal showpiece, now an open area which the local community can be proud of having fought for and shaped. Queen's Park in 2009 is full of life. The tennis club is thriving, the Spa echoes to the sound of children's play and the leaking lake has been repaired. In the summer there is free entertainment for the children and families gather around the little café next to the sandpit. Cricket games spread across the grass and picnics are laid under the trees and on the bowling green. In winter the shouts of impromptu football games echo around, and when there is snow sledges come speeding down accompanied by cries of excitement. All though the year, rain or shine, the joggers and dog walkers make their rounds. Occasionally there are open-air performances of plays in the gardens of the Spa. On such evenings as dusk falls hundreds of people gather with blankets and picnics to be transported to the forest of Arden or the woods near Athens. As the light fades, bats fly through the trees, swifts whistle in the sky and a fox pads silently along the edge of the crowd. In the distance is the faint sound of traffic. Queen's Park is at peace.

The gazebo is all that remains of the grand Attree Villa. Even the marble statue shown of the Emperor Aurelius has now disappeared

Friends

The hurricane of 1987 did have one beneficial effect. The trauma brought together people concerned about the Park and led to the formation of the Friends of Queen's Park in 1988. They have been very effective in lobbying for improvements, such as repairing the lake and arranging for a local sculptor to use some of the fallen tree wood to make intriguing 'cannon ball' benches. A very successful Hundredth Birthday Party for the Park was held, with a re-enactment of the opening ceremony of 1892 when the keys were handed over to the Mayor of Brighton and the gates thrown open. The original key is kept in Brighton & Hove Museum and was on display on the day. The gates and railings are long gone but in their place a ribbon was cut. Later other smaller events were organised, but the group then more or less faded away.

Fire, Smoke and Mirrors, a celebration in Queen's Park, to mark the beginning of the Brighton Festival May 2009

In 2004 The Friends of Queens Park was born again with the same objectives - raising funds to assist the Park and keep an eye on developments. One aim is to involve the community in consultation on the long-term management of the Park. The Friends regularly help the Park Keeper on work-days and may sometimes be spotted in the Park on a Sunday morning cleaning the lake, planting trees or tending the Wildlife Garden. They also organise an annual and popular 'Fun Dog Show' and the 'Sunday in the Park' family festival, and are reviving the summer music and drama events. Plans for the future include revitalising the Wild Garden, improving signage around the Park and investigating the possibility of restoring the Fountain.

We are very grateful to the Friends who have allowed us to use much of the text from their earlier booklet of the same title, and have helped in the publication of this history of their Park.

Acknowledgements

Original text: Various Friends of Queen's Park, Lavender Jones, Mary Allison, Douglas d'Enno, Chris Lowe
Research: Lavender Jones, Sue Berry, Andrew Bradstreet, Joyce Collins, Sally Jeffery, Barry Pointon, Derek Burns
Editing and additional text: Derek Burns
Book design: Simon Montgomery, Selma Montford
Technical support: Computer Box
Photographic research: Kevin Bacon, Peter Booth, Lavender Jones, Duncan McNeil
Wildlife photographs: Chris Lowe, Jason Shallcross
Maps and documents: Lavender Jones, Henry Smith

with thanks to...
Many of the photographs are reproduced from the J S Gray collection with the kind permission of the Regency Society of Brighton & Hove. The Royal Institute of British Architects gave permission for the reproduction of drawings by Charles Barry. Two prints and a number of photographs have been reproduced with the kind permission of the Royal Pavilion and Museums (Brighton & Hove). The cover and the painting of Thomas Attree were reproduced with the kind permission of Howlett Clarke solicitors. The Argus, Peter Booth, Lavender Jones, Henry Smith, Robert Jeeves of 'Step Back in Time' have loaned photographs.

The 2009 edition of The Story of Queen's Park Brighton is published in collaboration with the Friends of Queen's by Park
Brighton Town Press 10 Clermont Road Brighton BN1 6SG UK
t:01273 509209 f:01273 502018 e:info@brightontownpress.co.uk
w:www.brightontownpress.co.uk
The Story of Queen's Park Brighton ISBN 1-901454-12-3 ©
Printed by Delta Press, Unit 1, Industrial House, Conway Street, Hove BN3 3LW

FURTHER BOOKS AVAILABLE FROM US

Blighty Brighton: about Brighton in the First World War (1991)
ISBN 0-904733-55-6 @ £4.95
Past & Present: the Story of Blaker's Park (1994)
ISBN 0-9522856-0-6 @ £5.00 published by the Friends of Blaker's Park
The Vanishing Villas of Preston & Withdean (1996).
ISBN 1-901454-00-2 @ £5.50
Memories and Photographs of Brighton in the 20s & 30s (2002).
ISBN 1-901454-05-3 @ £6.99.
Preston : Downland Village to Brighton Suburb (2004)
ISBN 1-901454-07-X @ £9.99
Rose Hill to Roundhill : a Brighton Community (2004)
ISBN 1-901454-08-8 @ £9.99
The Landscape Book of Brighton Prints (2005)
ISBN 1-901454-07-X @ £14.99
Backyard Brighton: (2007)
ISBN 978-1-901454-10-9 @£12.75 (second edition)
Hilly Laine to Hanover : a Brighton Neighbourhood (2007)
ISBN 978-1-901454-11-6 @ £9.99

All books are available either:
via the website: www.brightontownpress.co.uk paying by Paypal
or by emailing: info@brightontownpress.co.uk
or by writing to: 10 Clermont Road Brighton BN1 6SG enclosing a cheque

They are usually also available at the following shops:
Books for Amnesty Bookshop, 15 Sydney Street Brighton.
Borders, Churchill Square.
The Pavilion Shop, Brighton Museum Shop and History Centre .
City Books, 23 Western Road Hove.
Kemp Town Books, 91 St George's Road Kemp Town.
Step Back in Time, 125 Queens Road Brighton.
British Bookshops and Stationers plc, Brighton and Hove branches.
Waterstones, corner of North Street and West Street.

The following post and packing charges should be added to the prices quoted Within the UK: £2 for one book, £3.00 for 2 or more books
Within Europe: £3.00 for one book, £4 for two or more books
Outside Europe: £4 for one book, £5 for two or more books, surface mail

All Cheques payable to 'Brighton Town Press'